THE TRAPDOOR TO HALLOWEEN

WRITTEN AND ILLUSTRATED BY
MARTIN RICHMOND

PublishAmerica
Baltimore

First printing

ISBN: 1-4137-6241-7
PUBLISHED BY PUBLISHAMERICA, LLLP
www.publishamerica.com
Baltimore

Printed in the United States of America

Dedicated to Sheila,
an enchantress who stole my heart and soul.

Ghostly good wishes

Martin Richmond

2005

Acknowledgements

Jacqueline, Ryan, Graeme, Kelly, Aimi and Fraser—wondrous children of vision and inspiration.

The Falkirk Writer's Circle for championing the creative urge to put pen to paper.

PublishAmerica for being there to turn my vision into reality.

Alex Burt and Fraser Shepherd for their technical wizardry.

CONTENTS

INTRODUCTION
11

MYTHS AND LEGENDS

MONSTERS AND DEVILS

GHOSTS AND ALIENS

THE WEIRD AND MYSTERIOUS

iNTRODUCTION

The Trapdoor to Halloween leads you into a world of ghoulies, ghosties, long leggedy beasties and things that go BOO! in the night. This poetic adventure takes you down a flight of cellar steps into the cloak of darkness, allowing you to carry only a flickering candle with you to the deepest recesses of the time of the year known as HALLOWEEN.

Ignore the blood curdling yells as you descend the rickety wooden staircase. Brush away all the cobwebs that cling to your face as a hundred tiny scampering legs swarm across your skin, seeking somewhere warm to hide. You shake them off and collecting your composure, continue down. The staircase is steep and creaks with each footstep as the light from the open trapdoor above becomes fainter and you descend deeper and deeper.

A scurrying, scratching noise below you in the blackness beyond the glow of the candle almost hides the chatter of several faint voices. Curiosity keeps you going slowly down, although fear scrapes incessantly at your heart!

Drops of liquid splash into your eye and as you wipe them away you wonder is it water, or blood? You're almost there, the handrail has a sticky, slimy feel to it and the smell of something rotten grows revoltingly stronger. Suddenly the trapdoor above you slams shut with an almighty BANG and the candle's flame goes out. Something or someone grasps your hand and you try to cry out but icy fingers touch your lips, urging you to silence.

Cracked voices echo across the cellar, whispering the words of a tale told in rhyme. You take a deep breath to listen but dare not exhale as you know that the creatures down here are listening too.

MYTHS AND LEGENDS

THE PIRATE'S GRISLY TALE

T'was on a filthy night such as this,
when the thunder gave the clouds a kiss
and lightning branched the heavens wide
to silver the tears it could not hide.
As the moon fought the clouds to glimpse
a murderous scene to force it to wince
and wish that it had never really tried
to see how it was that the pirate died?
When Captain Kraken made a pact with Hell,
a devil with a devil's soul to sell,
and crewed his sailing ship, *The Iron Demon*,
with thirteen skeletons instead of seamen.
He plundered the oceans turning them red
taking treasure and pleasure leaving dead
the crews and passengers of cargo ships
tearing off their very flesh in strips.
Man, woman and child, showing mercy for none,
shredding souls for the devil to feed upon.
The tyrant, Kraken, drove his crew with fear
to massacre night and day for o'er a year,
Toiling endlessly, scrubbing bloody decks
of an abattoir afloat in a Sargasso of wrecks.
But a hostile mutiny now showed its hand

from the thirteen pirates of his bony band
who rebelled against the Captain's view
that rest was not for a skeleton crew?
They seized their captain and carried him high
up the gusting rigging ignoring his cry
of, "Unhand me, blackguards, let me go,"
they impaled him above the nest of the crow.
Pierced upon the masthead still barely alive
a lightning bolt struck, splitting him wide.
and blasting his motley, rebellious crew
to the four winds as they furiously blew.
The ship sailed on and I'm told is sailing still
as a ghost, *The Iron Demon*, with an icy chill
reminder to pirates who hire devils to shout it,
"GOOD CREWS ARE HARD TO COME BY,
MAKE NO BONES ABOUT IT!"

RIDDLE OF THE MUMMY

Rameses the third, an Egyptian pharaoh
of three thousand years ago,
awoke with a splitting headache
and a desperate need to go.

He frantically needed the bathroom,
he was busting to go very soon.
So pushing off the lid of his sarcophagus
he glanced round the walls of his tomb.

He remembered taking a sleeping draught
and going straight off to his bed.
They shook him when he failed to wake up
so mistakenly presumed he was dead!

Thinking he must have passed away
he was mummified and placed in a tomb.
He awoke in a darkened museum
but thought he was still in his room.

The full moon shone through the skylight
lighting up Rameses the third,
who stumbled across the marble floor
unable to utter a single word.

Rameses peeked through a doorway,
he still needed to get some relief.
Clutching his dangling bandages he strutted,
tensely clenching his crumbling teeth.

He came to the top of an unlit staircase
spiralling away down three floors.
His wrappings tangled and down he tumbled
screaming out with muffled roars.

He hurtled down the stairway, cartwheeling,
bouncing from the banister to the wall.
He came to rest with a resounding crash,
at the foot of the stair in the hall.

The curator found him next morning
his yellowed bandages all in a muddle.
As dead as an ancient Egyptian should be,
and seated in a great big puddle!

THE LEGACY OF KING MIDAS

The golden medallion of King Midas
was lifted from sand beneath his tomb.
The native digger who found it
turned golden yellow in the gloom.

His pal, an experienced digger,
about as greedy as the first.
Solidified his friendship,
in a sudden glittering burst.

Within two days the entire crew
of the excavation was gold.
Except Sir Simon Truscot-Potts
who was stuck in bed with a cold.

When word spread about the medallion
the Egyptian army moved in.
They now have two shiny yellow tanks,
gold soldiers and a war they can't win.

Sir Simon soon left his sick bed
to survey all the 24-carat crowd.
Hordes of golden people, he thought,
I wonder if melting down humans is allowed?

He had the gold removed and sold
and had a grand palace built.
He bought everything he'd ever wanted
without any lingering gilt!

He didn't need to lift the medallion
he left it right where it lay.
And if he needed some extra cash
he sent a butler with a tray.

Butlers were ten a penny,
they were quite easy to find.
Now they were worth their weight in gold,
especially the trusting kind.

They say money doesn't buy happiness
his wife Goldie would certainly agree.
That's if she could talk she would say so,
but then silence is golden you see!!

GORGON STYLE

Onto the threshold the lady glided in,
in from the dark, rain swept street.
The hooded cloak hid the features
of a person you would not like to meet.

Miss Carol Ann, the hairdresser,
preoccupied gestured towards a chair.
The lady sat and threw off her hood
revealing her fearsome glare.

Mrs. Pringle looked up from a magazine
and turned a darker shade of grey.
Mrs. Burdge glanced from her hairdryer,
her complexion resembling clay.

Miss Carol Ann, without turning round,
waved her assistant across.
"Finish this lady off now Kelly?"
you could tell that she was the boss.

Mrs. Medusa walked forward and
when Miss Carol Ann called out, "Next,"
she seated herself at the mirror,
Miss Carol Ann looked perplexed.

Gazing at the writhing, hissing scalp
Miss Carol Ann scratched her ear.
"I'm sorry you're in the wrong place," she said,
"the petshop's next door my dear!"

THE HEADLESS HORSEMAN COMETH

Beware the lonely traveller,
walking in New England's woods,
a terrifying sight will gallop by,
chilling the warmest of bloods.

On a fiery, wild black steed
the headless horseman appears,
without any warning he charges,
his sword swinging as he nears.

It will sever your foolish head
clean from off your shoulder,
no worry of getting grey hair,
you won't be getting any older.

The swish of blood-soaked blade,
the demon hoof beats closing in,
you toss a coin to escape death,
heads you lose, beneath the chin.

The horrific, headless horseman,
once rode this trail, a poor stranger,
he ignored the signs beside the road,
BEWARE, LOW BRANCHES, DANGER!

KEEPING AN EYE OUT FOR THE CYCLOPS

The explorer discovered the Cyclops' lair
hidden far away from man.
Trapped in a cage he vented his rage
at the explorer's master plan.

"How did you find me?" he bellowed,
his single orb blinking at the sky.
"It was easy," said the explorer,
"it's in the phonebook under i."

"I should have gone ex-directory,"
said the Cyclops with dejection.
"I'd have found you anyway,
your optician has your glass
for collection."

"Other tell-tale hints and tiny clues
led me to your door today."
"Like putting, 'Mr C.Y. CLOPS,'
on your letterbox,
was a bit of a dead give-away."

"What happens to me now?"
the Cyclops wailed.
"I don't want to be locked in a zoo."
"Don't worry Cy," said the explorer,
"I've a job as a private eye for you."

THE TRUE STORY OF JACK AND THE BEANSTALK

It was soon after Jack had planted his beans,
not Heinz, but magic and you know what that means?
A giant plant sprouted, pushing tendrils to the sky.
even walking into town you could see it on high.

Jack popped into the local supermarket
for a carton of skimmed milk for his mum.
Since he'd sold the cow for the beans
he was rubbing a rear that was numb.

Gazing up he swore it was much closer
than the huge plant had been before,
and watched it come nearer and nearer
to the car park of the store next door!

Frantically he ran westwards it followed,
running to the south, it came too.
Hour upon hour it shrubbornly chased him,
and the higher the damn thing grew!

He collapsed on a park bench exhausted,
several miles away from his home.
"Those bloody magic beans," he said to himself,
"why won't this plant *leaf* me alone?"

Each day its shadow covered him,
blotting out the sun as he walked.
If only Jack had known the truth
and realised that he had been stalked!

YE OLDE SNICKET MONSTER

In the historic English city of York,
where Vikings pillaged and Romans walk,
exists many dark and narrow alley
in which you should not wish to dally.
The alleys, or snickets as locals say,
between buildings avoid the light of day.
Due to its slender width, so very narrow,
walking singly chills the very marrow.
Somewhere between its start and end,
some go missing; you may lose a friend.
Snatched in the Snicket monster's grip
none ever live to recount their trip.
Whisked away to who knows where,
leaving not a trace to its lair.
Its voracious appetite knows no bounds,
its gnashing teeth are echoing sounds?
No blood spatters just scratches on a wall,
show that it even exists at all.
Those who vanished into thin air,
never screamed as its talons tear.
We know it's there and where it lurks,
in Snicket shadows it silently works.
Taking the stragglers in mid breath,

introducing them to their own death.
The Vikings knew it, the Romans too,
the Victorians even tried to catch it
but we just haven't got a clue,
where it came from or where it hides
but Yorkies avoid the Snicket's sides.
The tourists in their thousands flock,
providing monster snacks round the clock,
so please avoid the alleyways if you can
to halt the Snicket monster's master plan.
To tear and rip, spindle and mutilate,
to eradicate all trace and seal your fate.
Visit York and wallow in its historic past
but avoid the Snickets or the visit will be…

…your last!

DRAGONMEAT

Ryan Jones the butcher had a roaring trade,
his customers queued around the clock.
A short while ago he couldn't sell anything,
no blood stained his butcher's block.

Ever since he started selling Dragonmeat
his fortunes were really on the mend.
The succulent barbecued steaks,
were sending people round the bend.

A dark-suited gent with a briefcase
poked his nose into the shop.
"You can't do it Mr. Jones," he said,
"keep it up and I'll call a cop!"

"Why, what's wrong, what have I done,
where's the bleeding crime?"
Mr. Jones stopped in mid chop,
of a rib that was dragonishly prime.

"You're selling meat described as Dragon,
when there's really no such thing,"
the gent from the Health department squeaked
as though he was about to sing.

"It *is* Dragonmeat and I can prove it,
just slither round the counter and follow me."
Mr. Jones trotted out to the back yard
carrying a large cellar key.

Down the dark cellar steps they trooped,
Mr. Jones was leading the way.
The Health man was close on his heels
not really knowing what to say.

They finally reached the cellar floor
walking down a passage dimly lit.
They came to a door at the end
and Mr. Jones said, "This is it!"

He opened the creaking oak door
and switched on a solitary light.
There, sat in the corner, was a dragon,
yes, a real dragon, that's right.

The man couldn't believe his eyes,
the creature was scaly green, and snoozing.
"Well," said Mr. Jones, "are you happy,
now that I've proved what we're using?"

"Hold on," said the man in the suit,
carefully putting his briefcase down.
"How can you be selling Dragonmeat,
when there's only *one* to be found?"

"Oh yes," said Mr. Jones strolling over
and tapping the dragon on the tail.
The dragon leapt up and belched flames
over the gent, turning dark red from pale.

The suit was burned right off him
and his body was charcoal roasted.
Mr. Jones produced a meat cleaver
and very loudly he boasted.

"I didn't say it was *made* from dragons
only that it was *dragonmeat*!"
You're the fifth Health man we've had
and you're all going down a treat!"

THE SWEET TOOTH FAIRY

Does anyone know what happens when
the Tooth Fairy's tooth falls out?
Is there a back-up squad
from the land of nod,
just what are these fairies all about?

Do fairies have teeth and if so,
is there a fairy dental scheme?
Are there little pillows
for the flighty fellows,
to hide a loose molar in a dream?

Do they get a gold or silver coin
left for the tooth that has decayed?
Do they even floss
to prevent the loss,
where is fairy toothpaste made?

If they eat nothing but fairy cakes
their teeth would never harden.
All fairies would be fat,
can you imagine that,
bulging from the bottom of your garden!

Fairy dentists can't use smelly gas
or needles that might sting.
Make an appointment now,
they'll show you how,
go on, give the dentist a fairy ring!

When you wake up late one night
and you find your tooth has gone!
The fairy must have been
it wasn't just a dream,
when they pick up ev-fairy-one!

If you live way across the water
and of dentists you're quite wary.
Don't you fret,
your Mom will get,
a call out to the Cross Channel fairy!

THE CAMPAIGN AGAINST SANTA CLAUS

In the dead of night a fat, bearded fellow
slips very quietly into your home.
Carrying a sack, wearing a blood red suit,
AND YOU ALLOW THIS PSYCHO TO ROAM?

He leaves presents for your children
but never leaves one for you.
He comes and goes as he pleases,
why you let him I haven't a clue?

He doesn't enter by the front door,
he's really lost the plot.
His bulk squeezes down the chimney
whether you've got one or not!

Hooded, he skulks in the dark
eating mince pies and guzzling milk.
For all you know his underwear
could be black, frilly and silk.

The snow piles up on the ground
and he lands right on the roof.
Abusing reindeers till their noses glow,
WELL, DO YOU NEED MORE PROOF?

Don't trust this flying tub of lard
don't let this monster inside.
Why doesn't he let himself be seen,
what *has* he got to hide?

Is it a coincidence he rides a *sleigh*,
the misspelling of a serial killer?
Gaining your confidence he'll attack,
he's not just a stocking filler.

Don't forget he's got your lists
and he's checked them twice.
Really he's seeking out the naughty,
he's not interested in the nice.

He's a father without kids,
drives free transport through the snows.
He only works one day of the year,
I wonder if the IRS knows?

Join the campaign "Ban Santa Now"
before he commits an obscene act.
Don't let him get his clause in you,
come on, let's get this toy boy sacked!

NOT QUITE YETI

The mountain climbers halted
in their quest to reach the top,
of one of the bleak Himalayas,
a cold, inhospitable spot.

Two of the brave men stood,
consulting an open map,
the third removed his knapsack
and began to loosen the strap.

He sat midst the blanket of snow,
the frost fringed his beard with white,
his breath blew mist cross his vision,
through his gloves he felt the frost bite.

Before his eyes stepped a figure
about a hundred yards away,
its height was eight feet or more,
covered in a shaggy coat of grey.

Through its fur glinted two steely eyes,
its bear-like feet crunched the snow,
as it moved away down the slope,
the climber dumb-struck watched it go.

"It's the- the-" stuttered the climber,
pointing at the thing shuffling away.
"It's the abolb - the aboom - the ablomm,"
the word he just could not say.

The creature turned in his direction
its eyes were burning like hot coal.
It staggered frighteningly toward him
he felt a fear penetrating his soul.

Its foul breath clouded his cheeks
its hair close enough to brush.
It whispered with a finger to its lips
"Bin Laden says to you, *hush*!"

BELIEVE IN THE BEAST

Bemused, beguiled, bedraggled in bedlam,
beyond battlements blackened by bitumen,
between brandished broadswords battles are born,
the blood bathers breaststroke begins.
Baal bellowed at the brutes from above,
"Begone brave boys, blessed be the bountiful,
bestill the belligerence," he blazed .
But Beelzebub arose behind the boss' back,
blackening the brightness with black magic abound.
"I bestow a beast on you bedevilled brothers,
behold the Basilisk, biting far worse than its bark."
The behemoth with blazing breath belched,
over the bewildered blood-letters with bile.
Bodies burning, their bellicose souls beseeching,
were brought before the blackest bishop begging.
Branded and beaten, bones broken beyond time,
the basest being adds baubles to its bracelet.
Beware the "Bette noire" biding time,
laying bets the barbarians blow bad once more,
bringing the beast from beneath
Scotia's brooding Ness.

MONSTERS AND DEVILS

THE FEATURES OF SWAMP CREATURES

Deep in the Everglades heavy mist swirled,
a flock of birds, startled, broke the air.
Bursting from the swamp two figures arose,
green slime dripping from their hair.

They moved in perfect harmony,
ploughing chest high through the water,
matching each others reflective motion,
the watching moon in its last quarter.

Their gargoyle-like heads submerged,
their reptilian feet sliced through the air,
their mirror-image moves continued,
no terrifying display could compare.

Both creatures were pleased beyond measure,
with slime oozing mouths sickly grinning,
they knew they would win the gold medal,
for Swampland Synchronised Swimming.

FRANKENSTEIN'S MONSTER???

"IT'S ALIVE! IT'S ALIVE!" an electrifying cry,
illuminated by flashes of blue sparks.
High voltage burst through its body,
leaving ravaging scars and birth marks.

Steel bolts protruded from its neck
and from its tiny, exposed brain,
oozed a green, slimy, bubbling mess
where it had long since been lain.

Piece by piece, painstakingly made,
with most tender, loving care,
Stitching on each finger, toe and nostril
and gluing on every single hair.

Seven feet six in its stocking feet
the obvious pride of the creator.
Taking eagerly to life's tragic stage
with a Gothic castle as its theatre.

It cannot communicate with fellow man,
it grunts and snorts and mumbles,
walking awkwardly, as a new-born babe,
gradually learning as it stumbles.

We all know its true vocation,
its history, devious and sinister.
Its good intentions will end in misery,
just like every new Prime Minister.

ALONG CAME A TEN-TON SPIDER

Its web was attached to the guttering
of the corner of number four,
strung across the street to the lamp post,
down by the Green's front door.

It had been there since early morning,
well it wasn't there last night,
and judging by the cocooned milk float,
dawn would be about right.

The road-sweeping lorry was unlucky,
coming today of all days.
You don't usually see it for months,
then it comes along and it stays.

Old Mrs. Brown from forty-seven
must have been shocked indeed.
She takes her poodle for walkies early,
now all that's left is a lead.

The newspaper boy delivered his last
and won't be coming by again.
Read about it if you get your own paper,
or better still watch TV's *News at Ten*.

The fire brigade couldn't shift it,
all that's left is a great deal of water.
Police lost a squad car, three troopers,
a dog van,
and a long arm that's very much shorter.

Sheila poked her head out the window,
visibly shocked and all of a fluster,
rushing through the house and appearing,
wildly wielding a feather duster.

The battle was simply amazing,
nothing before or since had been seen,
but in less than it takes to boil a kettle,
spider and web were wiped clean.

Now the streets are quiet and deserted,
but it won't be staying that way,
the spider Sheila squished was called,
"Junior,"
and it's Mommy is coming to stay!

DE-BUGGED

Graeme Buffery dearly loved his work,
he dealt constantly with death you see.
The death of things smaller than himself,
in killing insects he'd earned a degree.
He owned a small firm called "DE-BUGs"
and a van inscribed with this prayer,
"DE – BUGS are DELETED
AND YOU'LL BE DELIGHTED,
by Buffery the ant empire slayer,"
A hard hat, goggles, overalls
and a backpack ready and rarin' to go,
down to the cellar on a hot humid day,
a damp darkness 'neath the wings of a crow.
The carrion descends spreading death
from a cylinder strapped to his back.
Tiny, shiny, carapace shells upturn
kicking thin air from the poisonous attack.
Their screams could not be heard,
above the laughter within his mask,
exterminating the tiny creatures,
delighting in his gruesome task.
Later seated at the foot of the steps,
his cylinder and mask placed at his feet,

he blew smoke rings across the killing field,
These things, he thought, *are easy meat*.
Music wafted through the cellar door
suddenly stopping as the news began.
He remembered the lottery ticket he'd bought,
could he be sitting here a very rich man?
The results were announced and mentally
he marked the numbers off one by one.
He had all six, HE HAD *ALL* SIX!
"I've won", he shouted, "I'VE WON!"
As he waved the ticket about on high
it was snatched from his fingertips.
He turned to see an enormous cockroach,
words simply just froze on his lips.
The cockroach, severing Graeme's head,
explained, "Every one was once a relation,
and this will do very nicely I think,
ten million dollars in compensation?"

THE BLOB

The awesome slime pulsated,
as it slithered across the floor.
It left a glistening trail behind
as it shuffled through the door.

It headed towards the kitchen,
splodging right through the hall.
A tabby cat arched its back
and scrambled right up the wall.

It squeezed beneath the kitchen door
and oozed its way inside.
It slimed up to the kitchen sink,
Mother, washing, almost died.

She screamed a blood-curdling yell
at the thing that drove her mad.
"Get down off there now young man,
or I'll go and tell your Dad."

Mommy blob was very angry
with her naughty little child,
but it only wanted to know how,
she kept her washday hands so mild?

A DEVIL OF A JOB

The bankrupt face of Mr. Hull
was cradled in both his hands.
He'd lost everything he'd owned,
stocks, shares, money, land.

He wept pitifully over his desk,
which he didn't even possess,
his tears splashed down into his beer
which he foolishly drank to excess.

He bemoaned his run of bad luck
and all the chances he'd lost,
the dirty deals that'd gone sour
and the friends he'd double-crossed.

Definitely not a pleasant man,
devoid of morals or good deeds,
supposing blood was solid gold,
he'd find a stone that bleeds.

"I'd sell my soul in a minute,"
he sobbed and cried out loud,
"To be rich once more again
and be better than the crowd."

His office door crashed open,
thick black smoke poured right in,
the tremendous heat singed his eyebrows
and scorched his double chin.

"I'll be burned to a crisp," he said,
"I just don't want to die."
But the smoke vanished instantly
and he wiped a tear from his eye.

Framed in the doorway, a man in black,
black cape, black shirt, and black gloves,
he reminded Mr. Hull of a magician,
about to conjure up doves.

The man in black removed his hat
and loosened a scarf at his throat,
Mr. Hull was startled to stay the least
at the horns protruding like a goat.

"I am here at your request, Mr. Hull,"
said the satanic looking man.
"You offered your soul for sale,
take a look at my guaranteed plan."

He produced a scroll from his pocket,
scorched and heavily steaming.
"Sign this now and make your wish,"
his jagged teeth blackly gleaming.

"W-wish, anything?" he stammered,
trying hard to read the small print.
"Whatever your heart desires my friend,"
his oily eye winking an evil glint.

"Okay Mr. Lucifer, you've got a deal,"
said Mr. Hull scribbling his name.
"A billion dollars right here, right now,
legal, tax free, and won in a game."

"No problem sunshine, there you go."
that's where Mr. Hull's life ceases.
For he got the billion dollars as promised,
when he drowned in ten cent pieces.

THE PLANT MAN

The doctor's surgery door burst open,
a man stood screaming in panic.
"DOCTOR, YOU'VE GOT TO HELP ME!"
The doctor jotted down, "manic."

"Calm down," soothed the doctor,
"just sit down now, please"
The man clad in hooded anorak
began to cough and wheeze.

"How can I help you, Mister…er?"
a hood completely masked the strange man.
"It's Triffid," he said, throwing back his hood.
the doctor gasped and nearly ran.

Mr. Triffid's head was a tangled bush,
of matted leaves, branches and thorn.
Vines sprang from his ears and nostrils
around his neck grass grew like a lawn.

Shocked and stunned the doctor spoke
quite unsteadily at first.
"Good grief man, I thought I'd seen it all
but this…this is the worst."

He composed himself and apologised.
"Sorry old man, it was the shock."
"I understand," said Mr. Triffid,
"don't worry about it Doc."

"You'd better get undressed," the doctor said,
not really wanting to see more.
But when Mr. Triffid shed his clothing
the doctor fainted on the floor.

Moss-covered fingers glistening with dew
mopped the Doc's fevered cheek,
The doctor awoke after dreaming,
that he had performed CPR on a leek!

"Mr. Triffid, you're a medical marvel,"
said the doctor sitting back in his chair,
he swatted away the clouds of greenfly
that swarmed from Mr. Triffids hair.

"I don't know what to do," he said,
"it's quite worrying and queer?"
"I understand," said the doctor,
"let's get to the root of the problem here."

"Maybe it could be hereditary,
a branch of your family tree?"
Mr. Triffid wasn't moved at the sarcasm,
as the doctor could plainly see.

"I think this will pass quite soon,
you appear to be deciduous."
"At least when autumn comes
you won't look quite so ridiculous!"

"So I'll give you a course of tablets,
take them three times a day."
"Will it cure the condition?" Triffid said.
"No, but it'll keep the greenfly away!"

ZOMBIELIEVABLE

The cemetery earth erupted
as all the living dead arose,
dragging their rotting bodies up,
spilling soil from their ragged clothes.

They staggered from their resting places,
away from their headstone and tomb,
down the hill they trooped together,
silhouetted by a harvest moon.

The mass of corpses surged together
pouring out through the cemetery gate,
strutting towards a lamp-lit house,
the few living unaware of their fate.

They shattered doors and burst windows,
as screams of terror rent the air.
A family cowered in the living room,
frightened like mice in their lair.

Flesh-crumbling arms outstretched,
the stance of a maniacal killer,
a zombie lunged to switch the TV on,
in time for Michael Jackson's *Thriller*!

WEREWOLF – WASWOLF – WHATWOLF

The full moon painted the woodland
a slick coat of eerie silver grey.
Something stirred in the undergrowth
its presence about fifty feet away.

I swiftly turned and ran in panic,
my heartbeat began to race.
Dashing through bushes and trees
branches whipped and scratched my face.

I gasped frantic for some air
my lungs were fit to burst,
close behind came a howl,
I now feared the worst.

My muscles ached fearfully,
my legs seemed to burn,
the growling came closer,
I didn't even dare turn.

A tree root tripped me,
I crashed to the floor,
I scrambled to my feet
and turning round I saw…?

There, before me silhouetted,
in the moonlight's spectral glow,
a face now quite familiar,
smiling wickedly, chuckling low.

As I stood panting and gasping
the figure laughed out loud.
"You nearly wet yourself there,
you soft, big girl's blouse."

The full moon beamed across
my brother's smirking face,
but the smirk seemed to vanish
as amazement took its place.

He staggered backwards shocked,
choking words he could not find,
He suddenly turned and ran,
I followed closely behind.

He thrashed panic-stricken away
through the bracken and the bush,
his clothing ripped by thorn and branch
unconcerned in a headlong rush.

He fell crumpled and exhausted
into a small clearing by a pool.
The full moon was glistening
its shiny reflection like a jewel.

A hideous, snarling howl hit the air
as I touched my sweating brow,
I touched only matted hair and growled,
"WHO'S WET HIMSELF NOW-
WOOOOOOOOO!"

JEKYLL AND HYDE POTION

Doctor Jekyll clutched at his throat,
his foaming glass dropped to the floor,
his features changed very rapidly,
his voice whispered into a roar.
His eyes bulged, blazing, bloodshot red,
fangs curved over his bottom lip,
hair sprouted rapidly across his cheeks,
evil had him in its vise-like grip.
The foul brew had done its trick,
his form changed from good to bad,
Mr. Hyde growled deep within his throat,
"It's the worst cup of tea I've ever had!"

COUNT CALORIES

A vampire who loved garlic bread,
found he feared spare ribs instead.
He went really weak at the knees
at the sight of hot dog with cheese
and ketchup just made him see red .

Sausages sent him into convulsion,
corned beef gave his bowels propulsion.
He developed toothache
from a veal pasta bake
and pork pies filled him with revulsion.

Salami caused him to shiver and shake,
a lamb chop made his nerves quake.
But what upset him for sure,
was the curse's only cure,
of impaling his heart with a steak,
(Gammon, of course.)

VAMPIRE SPOTTING

I could tell at a glance that the man was strange,
not really a human at all.
Stood in the bus shelter, waiting for the 43,
just him and me, that's all.

Maybe it was the flash of yellow in his eyes
that most probably gave him away,
or maybe the long black cloak he wore,
that made me not want to stay?

Or possibly his pale white, sunken cheeks
and that nasty, leering grin,
or the long, bony, wrinkled fingers
that scratched his thin, pointed chin?

It was probably his sickly smile
exposing his sharpened teeth,
or maybe the way he just floated,
the ground not meeting his feet.

Whatever it was I found distasteful
was solved by giving him a push,
because not even the Prince of Darkness
can suck blood from the wheels of a bus!

A CHRISTMAS TALE FROM THE DEVIL'S DISCIPLE

Oh hell, it's Christmas again,
the boss is a devil to please,
come to think of it he *is* the devil
and he hates all Christmas trees!

I'll nip up to the shops in my break,
and buy him something really nice.
I can't get much on a disciple's wage,
well, everything's such a hell of a price!

Charging through the shopping mall
with my credit card at the ready,
I get a present pretty quickly,
I do hope he'll like the teddy?

I stop off for a Cornish cream tea
at the quaint, Olde Willow tea-room,
it's quiet after those demon shoppers
tearing around to meet their doom.

They don't seem to really mind
my pungent, acrid, sulphur smell,
but the pot of tea and bran scone
certainly went down extremely well.

I suggest to the manager, Jacqueline,
she should do something really spicy,
so in negligee she leaps on the table,
suddenly my presence seems very dicey.

I pay the bill and leave a tip,
"Don't back the horses," I say!
Boss disagrees 'Cos he likes a bet,
especially on Boxing Day.

I get back to work at long last,
making lists of evil people and places.
I add shopping malls to the very top
and shop assistant's with sour faces!

I sneak Satan's gift, tied with tinsel,
right inside his stinking woolly sock,
too bad he was wearing it at the time,
it gave him quite a yule tide shock.

He screamed abuse at me for the prezzie,
he say's teddies are useless slime,
but I noticed he put it on his pillow
to snuggle up to at beddy-boo-boo time!

JAWS RETURNS

The black tail fin was unmistakable
a great white shark was abound,
screams tore through the air like thunder
with a dun-dun-dun-dun sound.

Electrifying panic fuels the soul
with a survival maddening dash,
don't dare to look behind you
you don't want to be that rash.

You might need a bigger boat
or have to close the beaches
when you see the monster's jaws
and how far its bite reaches!

Its rows of vicious teeth gleam
as the bather's blood runs icy cold,
but Olympic records would be broken,
now swimmers have incentive for gold!

GHOSTS AND ALIENS

HAUNTED HOUSEFULL

"BOO!" he shouted loud and clear,
enough to frighten the dead,
Mrs. Proudfoot wasn't at all pleased
and swiped at Mr. Proudfoot's head.

"It was only a joke," he whined,
pretending to rub his ear.
"You'll be wishing you were dead,"
she said, "if you do it again my dear."

The couple were viewing at night
their newly purchased house,
a creaking old mansion, still occupied,
by something much scarier than a mouse.

Agatha Proudfoot pushed a disapproving finger
through dust an inch thick on the stair,
a shadow moved on the landing above,
Agatha tutted and was not aware.

The spooky staircase loomed upwards,
its banisters ornate in the gloom,
the night sky flashed with lightning,
silhouettes danced in the rooms.

They moved from room to room,
Agatha muttering all the while,
George shook his head at Agatha
as her language grew very vile.

"A pig in a poke you've saddled us with,
you good-for-nothing worm.
You even crashed the car on the way here,
do you think we've got money to burn?"

"Of course not, my dear," said George,
trying to ignore her nagging again,
he also ignored creaking floorboards above
and the clanking of a ghostly chain.

Agatha screamed a bloodcurdling yell,
when a cat appeared at her feet.
It arched its back, hissed and spat,
cat and Agatha's heart skipped a beat.

The cat vanished through a cat flap,
moving like its tail was on fire.
Agatha shouted to George in the kitchen,
her voice getting higher and higher.

"What's wrong now, seen a ghost?"
said George sarcastically waving his arms.
"Ghosts simply do not exist," said Agatha,
wiping cold sweat from her palms.

"Don't be a stupid fool George,
there's really no such thing,
Next you'll believe in hobgoblins,
and tooth fairies dancing in a ring."

Suddenly a violent knocking
began pounding at the front door.
In the doorway stood an Avon lady
who screamed and hit the floor.

"What's wrong with her I wonder?"
Agatha said with a loud snort.
"I think," said George, "that accident we had
was worse than we had thought!"

A sudden realisation hit Agatha,
she swiped at George once more,
but when her hand passed through his head
she could feel her spirit soar.

"Our bodies must still be in the car,"
said George, "we're dead you see,
and as ghosts we must haunt our house,
so Agatha, it's a great big BOO, from me."

G-G-GHOST TRAIN

The car slammed through the doors
the way ahead was pitch black.
The doors crashed closed behind us
as we both hurtled over the track.

A skull lit up green before us
as screaming filled the air,
we held each other so tightly,
just waiting for the next scare.

An axe sliced down before us
as a severed head went flying by,
we rattled round another corner,
something lightly touched my eye.

A witch stirred a cauldron wildly
In a blood red flashing light.
In the darkness somewhere above us
screeching vampire bats took flight.

Our hands clutched, aching,
just barely coping with the fright,
when a luminous, hairy spider,
dropped suddenly into sight.

The exit doors burst open wide
to bright light and cool fresh air.
I glanced relieved at my companion,
but found, *there was no one there!*

A SÉANCE IS SUPPOSED TO BE SPOOKY

You know, I can see dead people,
spirits of those gone to a better place.
Those who hang around after death,
not wanting to leave the human race.

I myself held a séance one time,
six people seated round a table.
I invoked the spirits to descend
and speak to as many as were able.

To my right sat an enormous lady,
who seemed proud to be obscenely fat.
She dwarfed her husband beside her,
who resembled a bald tabby cat.

On my left sat a couple of ladies,
prim and proper and plain as can be.
As pale as two pints of semi-skimmed milk,
in leafy dresses, like silver birch trees.

The sixth sensible person round the table
was a man who had only one ear.
He had glasses that kept on slipping,
so he could only half-see and half hear!

Nothing occurred, no one appeared,
no knocks or voices were heard.
Disappointed I apologised to the visitors,
who began to leave, I felt absurd.

As I showed them to the door
another five people were there?
I turned back to my first guests,
but they had vanished into thin air!

The ghosts *had* attended the séance,
no wonder they didn't answer my calls.
I felt an icy ripple run right over me,
my skin grew goosebumps and crawled.

The ghosts that came and went,
made me feel so very much afraid,
but I can't allow spooks to a séance,
who weren't invited and hadn't even paid!

TRAVELLING GHOST TO GHOST

Through a solid brick wall of the Old Inn
the figure appeared, a translucent, sickly grey.
The ghost detective switched on his camera
turning this blackest night into day.

The ghost stopped and stood quite still
slowly raising up a skeletal hand.
"No publicity please," it screeched,
"but a passport photo would be grand."

"I'm going on vacation very soon,"
it announced, poking the gap in its hood.
"You see, I go where the spirit takes me,
and they say haunting in Scotland is good."

"You can't leave," the investigator squealed,
"I haven't yet proved that you exist!"
"Don't worry," said the ghost departing,
"you're next on the INN-SPECTRE'S list."

MOON MAN

Stepping out of the spacecraft
I faced a dark silent world.
Striding across the landscape
I watched as my planted flag unfurled.

My solo mission to set foot
on the moon's surface had begun.
The Earth glowed brightly above me
like a pale blue reassuring sun.

All contact with Earth had ceased
I was there entirely alone.
I talked to myself in the silence,
there was no one around to phone.

The moon dust lifted each small step,
floating before settling down.
I moved slowly from the module
but something made me frown?

I looked back at my footprints
perfectly formed in the dust.
And noticed a new set of prints
my heart was set to burst.

I turned my helmet-encased head
from left to right and behind.
The emptiness was truly eerie.
who, or what, would I find?

Prints were scattered around me,
I stepped back truly aghast.
I saw a picture of my Mom
taken the summer before last.

The prints had fallen from my pocket,
all of them my photo's from home.
Collecting them up I was handed one,
Good grief! I WAS NOT ALONE!

Falling over backwards I gazed up
at a blue scaly creature that barked.
Apparently my lunar module,
It said, was illegally parked!

I had to shift it now, immediately
or it would have me towed away.
I dropped my trousers and mooned it,
and then it promptly ran away!

A STAR HAS LANDED

The traffic in the high street halted,
heads turned amazed and shocked,
a spacecraft had landed in the road,
all vehicles around were blocked.

A door hissed open by the pavement,
a weird masked figure began to show.
It staggered slowly from its doorway
bathed in a throbbing, eerie glow.

A shout went up, smiles broke out
the bleached creature met the throng.
It removed a single sparkling glove,
OH NO, Michael's going to sing a song!

WE ARE NOT ALONE

The loneliness and solitude,
the madness of standing still,
the isolation of ignorance,
the stubbornness of human will.

Our arrogant superiority
sitting on this speck of dust.
When friends are somewhere out there,
if we could only learn to trust.

The abject refusal to admit is
that mankind is not really alone,
in the great expanse of endless night,
someone's hanging on the phone.

Imagination stretched to breaking point,
boundaries twinkling in the eye.
Tease that thought a little further,
to the point where answers lie.

What is not understood
is discounted and dismissed.
The love of life is cherished
then discarded with a fist.

Doubting whether they come in peace
is to show the unknown our fear.
But their appearance may be human,
and they *already* could be here.

Question our human existence,
question what friendship is worth .
Ask yourself if the poet of this piece,
is really of this earth?

TO BOLDLY GO

We're plotting our way across the stars,
a careworn passage of dreams,
riddled with reason to hold back time,
in space no one cares if you scream.

The eclipse round the ear of endless night
throws a corona across the moon,
the guiding light points straight to heaven
its boundaries breached by thought balloon.

A comet's tail paints the heaven's curtain
with a brush stroke deep and wide,
the darkness swallows its passing
as the cosmos allows it to hide.

The earth shrinks away like a pebble
dropped away into a murky sea,
a wink of recognition from our shore
then home is gone and so are we.

The distant dog star beckons,
you cannot really be Cirrius?
We land and break out the picnic basket,
this vacation is gonna be delirious.

BORG-ANISATION

The metallic cube hove into view
all living creatures turned and flew.
No escaping the threat of the Borg nation,
outright slaughter or assimilation?
The former a far more preferable end
than a living death without a friend.
All thinking as one with single objective,
domination, and join the collective.
A fearsome horde of irresistible drones,
laying waste to planets, bleaching their bones.
But once a Borg, always a Borg, except a few,
Locutus became Picard, then there was Hugh!
Also the stunning form of Seven of Nine
saving Voyager's crew time after time.
She could be a cunning Borg plot,
returning to Earth and enslaving the lot.
But she and Data would get on fine,
both logical, methodical minds to combine,
producing little Borgettes, say four or five
and develop their crèche into a hive.
With little Spot One of Nine's metallic brow
glittering with lights like a Christmas tree now.

She's bound to go far beyond rank and file,
Whoops! She's said her first words –
"RESISTANCE IS FUTILE!!!"

THE TIME TO TIME TRAVELLER

Is this what they call déjà vu
or have I been here before?
I seem to recall
the clock on the wall
said three-fifty-five not five to four?

The machine flashes coloured lights
like a Christmas tree convention.
This is not the present,
the journey's not pleasant,
and I wish I'd not made this invention!

I've been and gone several times
in just a few scant seconds.
As my own time re-occurs
it whistles and it whirrs,
I think that my destiny beckons?

I return before I started out,
how can that possibly be?
I'm sitting over there
in my time travel chair,
and I'm staring right back at me!

I move the setting back again,
everything fades quickly away.
I arrive once more
to a crowded floor
and several of me are looking my way!

The room has become quite full,
I hear the echoes of my moans.
From all the me's
buzzing like bees,
I feel like I've sent in the clones!

I give up trying to go back,
there's no room left to move!
But a different face
has entered the place,
who on earth invited that Doctor Who?

THE WEIRD AND MYSTERIOUS

DEAD-END JOB

Twelve o'clock strikes, the midnight hour,
amid granite gravestone two men cower.
With spade in hand and lantern nearby
they set to work where dead men lie.
A saucer-eyed owl hoots his unrest
at finding these two unwelcome guests.
The earth is broken, a hole appears,
over this soil were spread many tears.
Soon their spades hit the wood below
and the dirt-covered coffin begins to show.
Wood splinters and cracks as the lid falls away
all bathed in the flickering lantern's ray.
The features of the corpse could now be seen,
a grim, crumbling face of mouldy green.
William Burke reached right down,
with the thoughts of a golden crown
but stopped as the death-dealing crook,
spotted the corpse held a blood red book.
Its eyes popped open, its stare was grim.
Its lips parted slowly dribbling down its chin.
"It's whispering!" the grave robber cried,
the other was silent, transfixed, terrified.
"Snap out of it man," he shouted at his friend,

the dead man lifted from his interrupted end.
A gurgle then issued of incoherent speech,
Burke stooped down as close as he dared reach,
He was close enough to see his dead eyes glisten
and held his breath just so he could listen.
Smelling the foul breath as the corpse spoke
cockroaches spilled forth distorting its croak.
His heartbeat raced, his fears were rife,
he heard the words,
"WILLIAM BURKE, THIS IS YOUR LIFE!"

THE STATUE THAT MOVED

"That statue, did you see it?" the man exclaimed,
his excited voice becoming pained.
"It moved, I saw it just then, didn't you?"
he said to the passers by as they flew,
wondering whether he should mention,
that its eyes had glared, right in his direction,
a menacing, threatening look, full of evil intention.
"No, I saw nothing," said a man, moving swiftly away.
"But it moved I tell you, please believe me, I pray."
A lady with a pram nodded at his wild claim,
muttering, "Deluded man, what a shame."
No one stopped, they all thought him mad.
Well a statue that moved, it's really quite sad.
He was totally alone, all about him had fled,
he looked up at the statue, was he off his head?
Seeing that no one believed his crazy tale
he climbed up on his stand turning stony pale.
"No one believes we exist," he whispered,
"we're as safe as safe can possibly be."
The other statue simply nodded and smiled
and both fell silent beneath the tree.

THE THING

The thing stepped in, I hid from view,
a hideous form, what shall I do?
From my vantage point behind the chair
I could see the fiend with its evil stare.

It moved on flimsy covered limbs,
the floorboards creaked each pace.
I could not bear to look upon
its ghastly, evil, pallid face.

Attack I must and launching forth
I see the thing does likewise.
It holds back when I hold back,
is this something that I recognise?

I wave a hand, it waves straight back
I'm beginning to understand,
why a tongue snakes out when mine extends
and knows all that I have planned.

It's not as ugly as I first thought
in fact it's good looking really.
If I switch on the light just now
I can see myself quite clearly.

VOODOO YOU DO?

Aimi Doolally plunged hatpins
viciously into the lifelike doll.
She muttered a few magical words
and threw it disgusted at a wall.

"Why won't it work?" she screamed,
"I've been trying it for weeks.
I enrolled at the Witches Night School,
but I've learned nothing from those freaks."

"I want to get rid of my husband, Fraser,
he's a right royal pain in the butt.
He's a boring wimp, he's a weakling,
with the charisma of a cashew nut."

"A little voodoo hex will see him away,
I'll send him six feet under!
If I can only perfect the magic words
I'll rip his useless guts asunder."

"I've been trying so very hard
It's given me a terrible pain.
It's a searing, burning sensation,
micro-waving my poor little brain."

"Now my legs are on fire, they're scorching,
tell me, what the hell is going on?
Fraser, Fraser, help me you twerp,
my toes are shrivelling, *they've gone!*"

Fraser stepped in with a long black cloak
wearing a starry conical hat.
"Yes Aimi dear, you screeched?
how can I help my little bat?

Aimi saw a doll in her likeness,
gripped very tightly in his fist,
she saw the pins protruding from it,
she couldn't speak, she just hissed.

"That night school I went to?" she croaked.
"Yes," said Fraser, "I also did it, *by post*."
"And you know I passed with flying colours,
so now Aimi my dearest—you're toast!"

THE FLAMES OF FEAR

The fire leapt from the fireplace
and danced around the floor.
It burned and singed all that it touched
and vanished right out of the door.
"MOM!" the child screamed in panic,
"COME QUICK!" she heard him shout.
She dashed to the living room,
and he said,
"WE NEED MORE COAL,
THE FIRE'S GONE OUT!"

HOT PROPERTY

The unpleasant Mr Taylor-Snyde
entered a posh clothing store.
His intent was to steal a new jacket,
to replace the old one he wore.

He tried on several styles until
he found one fitting just right.
He hung his old jacket in its place,
the old thing was getting too tight.

He boldly made straight for the exit
proudly wearing his stolen swag,
an assistant called out, "STOP THEIF!"
he'd forgotten to remove the price tag.

Down the escalator he sprinted,
feeling his temperature rise,
he assumed the chase made him hot
till smoke drifted past his eyes.

Through the revolving doors he ran,
customers and staff hot on his heels,
flames curled out from his pockets,
bursting out from his collar and sleeves.

His jacket was a ball of flame,
his head was glowing like a coal,
a girl called out "STOP, IT'S NOT A JACKET!
IT'S REALLY A BLAZER YOU STOLE!"

i COULD MURDER A BOWL OF CORNFLAKES

At midnight Rice Crispies were stabbed
and a box of porridge oats died the same.
A Weetabix gang were all strangled,
and Bran Flakes went up in flames.
A group of Sugar Puffs were drowned,
and some Cheerios met the same fate.
All killed, spindled and mutilated
in a display of milk-curdling hate.
WHODUNNIT, AND WHY,
police forces of the world are baffled,
with this gripping, nail-biting thriller.
They only know one thing for sure,
that it's the work of a cereal killer!

NOT QUITE DEAD, YET

The legions of those who passed away
stand on an escalator going down.
I cannot see the beginning of the line
and turning around I only frown.

The deadly line goes on forever,
of this hellish boredom giving queue.
Do I stand and watch these backs descend,
must I soon stand and fight a devil's crew?

An exploratory operation is commencing,
my life is hanging by a mere thread.
I feel knives penetrating my innards,
clutching a life raft in the sea of dead?

I died and now I return to the world
but the sleep, it consumes my will.
Perhaps the heinous crimes I committed
have been finally forgiven of me, still?

My eyelids are flickering seizing life,
I'm feeling such a hell of a lucky sod.
My eyesight returns within a blindfold
to hear the commands from a firing squad!

IT MAKES PEOPLE DISAPPEAR

On board the Bermuda cruise ship
a cabaret was well under way,
passengers were enjoying the band
as night parted company with day.

In the darkness they danced away
the jazz band was sizzling hot,
playing continuously till dawn
until suddenly they had to stop!

There was consternation in the band
playing Bermuda was as they feared,
they would need another musician now,
the guy on the triangle disappeared!

THE PAIN IS BACK

A policeman came across a troubled man
as he patrolled along his beat one night.
The man was acting in a strange manner,
appearing battling himself, in a fight.
As the policeman drew nearer he observed
the man violently struggling in vain.
with something attached to his throat,
inflicting some considerable pain.
"How can I help?" said the officer,
observing tentacles sprout from his back.
The man choked a strangled plea,
and the officer gave it a whack.
The blow his night stick inflicted
made the tentacles suddenly break free.
"Oh thanks," said the man clutching his spine,
"I've a bad back and it's fair killing me.

THE HOUSE OF HANGOVER

That searing clap of thunder
with lightning bolts of pain,
is a fierce, scorching forest fire
barbecuing kebabs on my brain.

But my headaches getting better.

Knitting needles dipped in acid
slowly skewer my fragile skull.
My eyeballs implode in boiling vitreous
while the china shop tackles the bull.

But my headaches getting better.

Hiroshima and Nagasaki roll together
into one big bang between my ears.
The bells of hell ring loud and clear,
oh, how that dark devil jeers.

But my headaches getting better.

Chalk screeching down a blackboard,
seagulls screaming at the sky.
The mournful cry of souls in torment
clamour mercilessly behind my eye.

But my headaches getting better.

Wait I see a glimmer of light
without a stabbing beam.
And I can finally touch my forehead
without it causing me to scream.

See, my headache's not going to win,
especially once the aspirin kicks in.

GIVE ME WINGS

I can do it,
I know I can fly.
With the aid of wings
I can accomplish things,
even drunken angels get high.

I want to be up there
between the white and the blue.
But the ravaging fear
is standing right here,
watching the boarding crew.

A phobic fence exists
keeping me from flight.
It will not beat me,
I'll not let it defeat me,
although my demons might.

A far off sunny clime
is well within my reach.
If only I don't refuse,
I should have the right to choose,
ain't life a cruel beach.

I'm up in the air,
swallowing sights I've never seen.
Breathtaking, awesome plumes,
of acres where cloud blossom blooms,
no countryside is this serene.

My minds aloft,
but my hearts still standing.
The world is open wide,
it's inviting me inside,
what's that about us landing?

TiME PiECES

The grandfather clock chimed midnight
quite loud and clear in the hall.
As the last chime struck and echoed away
the clock slowly moved away from the wall.

It edged its way along the carpet
rocking erratically from side to side.
It reached the living room door
and then nudged it open wide.

Lumbering forward into the room,
lined with clocks of every kind,
it seemed to stand in judgement,
attempting to make up its mind.

It turned to a royal carriage clock,
an antique owned by kings and queens.
The pendulum swung from its case.
smashing the time piece to smithereens.

Turning again it smashed a glass-domed clock
that exploded right across the room.
The long brass pendulum sliced like a sword,
scores of clocks soon met their doom.

An old wall clock chimed a protest
to stop this insane slaughter.
The grandfather clock ignored its pleas,
slicing it viciously into quarters.

A grandmother clock began ticking him off
asking why this destructive will?
He chimed he was bored stood in the hall
and just had plenty of time to kill!

HiTCH-CONCOCTiON
(a 21-movie tribute to Alfred Hitchcock)

The lady vanishes behind the torn curtain,
just a Paradine case of stage fright.
She left in a spellbound frenzy,
down thirty-nine steps in the night.

Blackmail was, without a shadow of a doubt,
the cause of poor Rebecca's vertigo.
I confess suspicion of her secret past,
to once being a notorious psycho.

She took up with entirely the wrong man,
yes, a man who knew too much.
The trouble with Harry was taxidermy,
you know, stuffing birds and such.

They met as strangers on a train,
on the North by Northwest line,
but the fat, bald man in the corner
had been lurking there all the time.

TRICK OR TREATMENT

The group of laughing children
hurried excitedly up the path.
A tooth fairy got to the bell first,
a tiny witch couldn't help but laugh

The chattering band formed a semi-circle
giggling with bags at the ready.
Impatient fingers stabbed the doorbell
but the door remained rock steady.

A light from the curtained front window
showed that someone was definitely in.
The sounds from a television echoed,
the doorbell battled against the din.

A junior Dracula kicked the door,
a mini-Mummy did likewise as well.
The patience of the trick or treaters
was wearing thin as the button on the bell.

The anger and frustration hit fever pitch
as the children assaulted the door.
Tears began as their voices escalated,
they just couldn't stand anymore.

The porch light suddenly came on
and the group fell silent as the grave.
An angry, elderly voice grew closer,
the row of masks tried to be brave.

The door swung open to an old man
waving a walking stick in the air.
"Get lost you little devils,
you'll get nothing here, I swear."

A Scream-masked child stepped forward
and raised his trick or treat bag.
"You cheeky little sod," said the old man.
stamping the floor like a wounded stag.

He knocked the bag to the ground
and lifted his stick over his head.
They didn't run away as he expected,
but held their ground instead .

He shouted at them, "GET AWAY."
they stood silent in their place.
He swung his stick at their heads,
a mask fell off, it hadn't got a face!

Though shocked he pulled at the masks,
ripping off every single one.
They all had blank expressions,
you see all of their features had gone!

His face went red, he began to choke,
he gripped his arm and chest.
Collapsing with a final tortured breath,
went face down on his silent breast.

The faceless children gazed down
at the lifeless form at their feet,
and pulling their stocking masks off
they all shouted, "TRICK OR TREAT!"

THE DEAD END

OH NO, it can't be, the end is nigh or is it?
Now that you've had your slightly scary visit,
will you see the darkness as only lack of light
or still think it hides only those things that bite?
I hope you find Halloween has much more,
so be brave when going through that door
and descending those steps just try and smile,
as not everything you might find is evil and vile.
This poet dedicated to *that* time of year
shows you that there's really nothing to fear,
except only what real fear itself can give,
so appreciate sweet life and live and let live!

POSITIVELY THE DEAD END!